CW00509775

GRADE **03**

SINGING

Songs & Teaching Notes for
Trinity College London
Exams 2018–2021

Includes CD of
piano accompaniments
and pronunciation guides

Published by
Trinity College London Press
trinitycollege.com

Registered in England
Company no. 09726123

Printed in England by Caligraving Ltd.

The Gartán Mother's Lullaby

Trad. Co. Donegal, Eire

Trad.
arr. David Wright

1. Sleep, O babe, for the red bee hums The

si - lent twi - light's fall. Ee - val from the Grey Rock comes to

wrap the world in thrall. *Á lían bhán ó* my child, my joy, My

love and heart's de - sire:_____ The cri - ckets sing___ you

2nd time to Coda ⊕

lul - la - by Be - side the dy - ing fire.

(dim. 2nd time)

mp

2. Dusk is drawn, and the Green Man's thorn Is wreathed in rings of fog.

p

pp

mp

poco più forte

Shee - vra sails__ his boat till morn U - pon the star - ry bog:_____ Á

p

lían bhán ó_____ the pa - ly moon Hath brimmed her cusp___ in dew,_____ And weeps to hear___ the sad sleep - tune I sing, O love, to you._____

D.C. al Coda

Coda

fire._____

El Vito

Trad.
arr. David Wright

Vivo ♩. = **72**

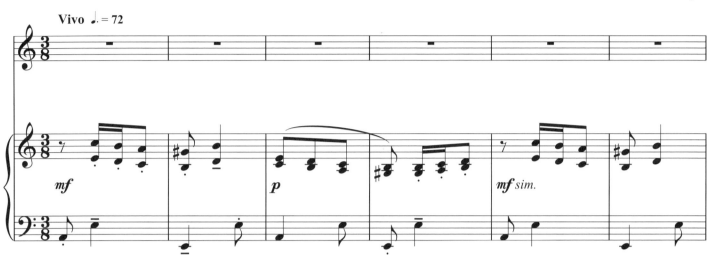

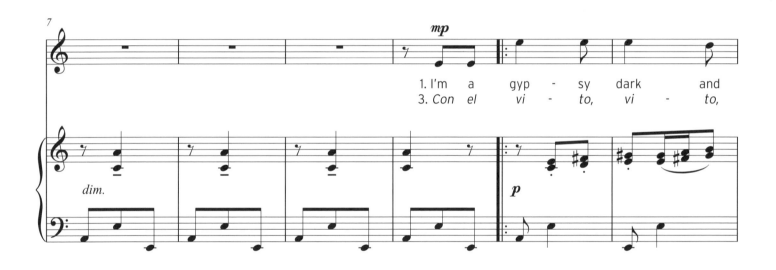

1. I'm a gyp - sy dark and
3. *Con el vi - to, vi - to,*

hand - some, And my clothes are all in tat - ters, I'm a
vi - to, Con el vi - to, vi - to, va,___ Con el

1.

5

2nd time to Coda ⊕

1. I've no mo - ney in my poc - ket, But my
3. When I've mo - ney in my poc - ket, Then per -

girl is by my side.
-haps I'll mar - ry you.

poco rall.

2. Now a

When I Was One-and-Twenty

A E Housman
(from *A Shropshire Lad*)

Cecil Armstrong Gibbs
(1889-1960)

When I was one-and - twen - ty I

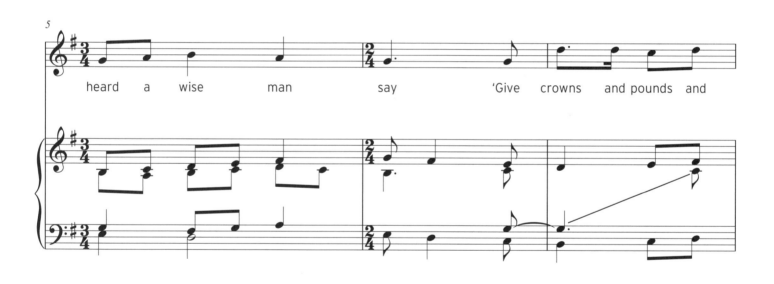

heard a wise man say 'Give crowns and pounds and

guin - eas But not your heart a - way; Give

heart out of the bo - som Was ne - ver given in

vain; 'Tis paid with sighs a - plen - ty And

sold for end - less rue.' And I am two - and -

-twen - ty, And oh, 'tis true, 'tis true.

Close Thine Eyes

King Charles I
(1601-1649)

Mary Plumstead
(1905-1980)

Close thine eyes____

____ and sleep se - cure, Thy soul is safe,____ thy bo - dy____

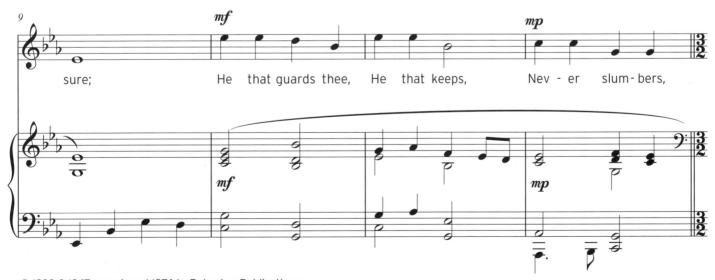

sure; He that guards thee, He that keeps, Nev - er slum - bers,

*Either version will be acceptable in the exam.

Come Sleep

John Fletcher

Peggy Glanville-Hicks
(1912–1990)

Come sleep, and with thy sweet de - ceiv - ing Lock____ me in de -

-light a while; Let some_ pleas-ing dreams be - guile All my fan - cies;

that from thence I_____ may feel an in - flu - ence_____

All my powers of care be - reav - ing.

Though but a sha - dow,

but a sli - ding Let_____ me know some lit - tle joy –

We_____ that suf - fer long an - noy Are con - ten - ted with a thought Through__ an id - le fan - cy wrought;

poco rit.

Oh let my joys have some a - bid -

a tempo

-ing.

The Apple Tree

Patricia Hackett

Miriam Hyde
(1913-2005)

The nod - ding lit - tle o-range tree With its fruit of gold and the sweets they hold Would lis - ten, lis-ten to__ me. Ah! be as gra-cious to me As the ap - ple, the ol-ive, the o-range tree, And lis - ten, lis - ten to___ me.

Peacocks

Ruth Dallas

Judith Exley
(b. 1939)

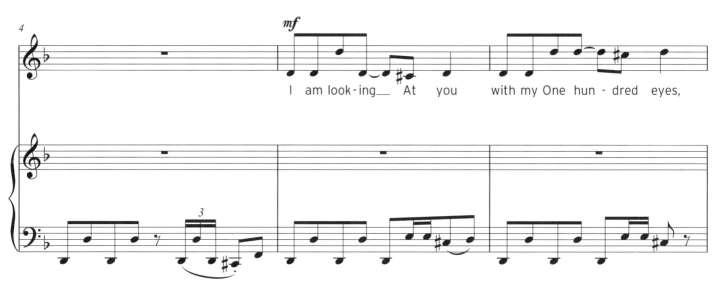

I am look-ing__ At you with my One hun - dred eyes,

said the Pea - cock, with his Tail spread, My eyes of sap - phire

I can't be both-ered by that now, Says the pea-hen.

Yes-ter-day A mouse ran a-long this wall And

if it comes a-gain to-day I'll nab it.

Lurking in the Pond

Kathleen Cowles

Colin Cowles
(b. 1940)

1. Frogs and toads and
2. Dra - gon - flies with

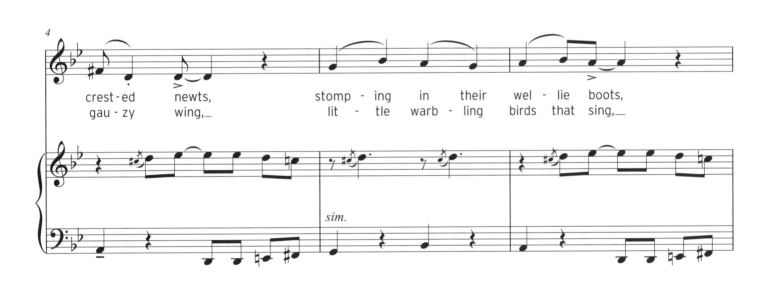

crest-ed newts, stomp-ing in their wel-lie boots,
gau-zy wing,_ lit - tle warb-ling birds that sing,_

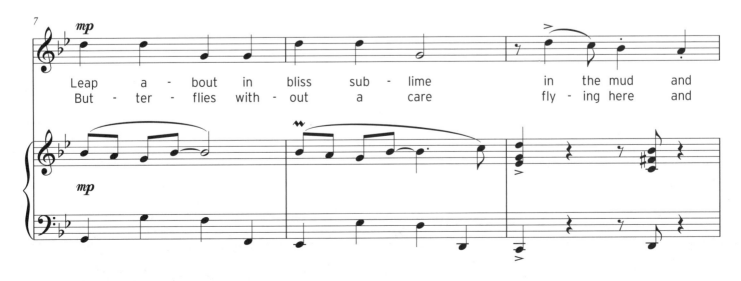

Leap a - bout in bliss sub - lime in the mud and
But - ter - flies with - out a care fly - ing here and

Oh yeah, oh yeah, oh yeah — Come and see__ what fun it can be:__ the pond is here for you__ and for me. (Boo, boo, bi, doo.)

24

for Grupo Vocal Olisipo

Irish Blessing

Trad.

Bob Chilcott
(b. 1955)

And un-til we meet a-gain,_____ may God hold you, may God hold_ you, ev-er in the palm_ of his hand._____

May the road rise to meet_ you,_____ may the wind be ev-er at your back, may the sun shine warm up-on_ your face, and the

Villanelle

Samuel Edenborough

Paul Harris
(b. 1957)

Moderato molto espressivo ♩. = 52   **rall.**   **a tempo**   *mf*

Oh

sempre legato

mf

con. Ped.

I've sailed this flat earth in a li - quor - ice yawl, I've sung

songs drink - ing rum on the thun - der - ing sea, and I've

cried to the stars for a mer - maid's___ call.

I've steered through the gloom on the teeth of a squall, while the sun sank its eyes and for - got a - bout me, Oh I've sailed this

fire, watch the dark - ness fall, and I'll think of the

gulls on the gusts as they flee: for I've sailed this flat

earth in a li - quor - ice yawl, and I've cried to the

stars for a mer - maid's__ call.__

From a Railway Carriage

Robert Louis Stephenson
(1850–1894)

Ian Higginson
(b. 1959)

Fast-er than fair - ies, fast-er than witch-es. Bridg-es and hou - ses, hed-ges and ditch-es; And

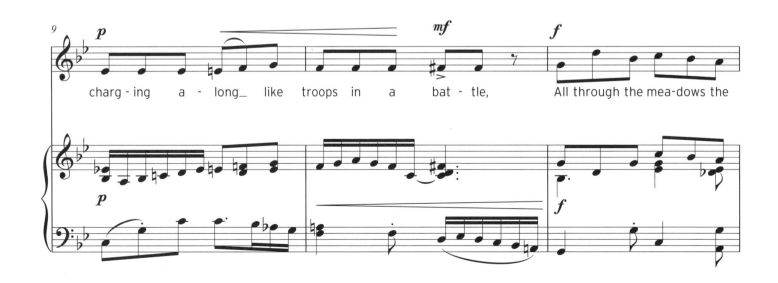

charg-ing a - long_ like troops in a bat - tle, All through the mea-dows the

-way in the road____ Lump - ing a - long____ with man__ and load; And here is a mill__ and there is a riv - er; Each__ a glimpse and gone_____ for ev - er!

Gone for ev - er!_____

Cool Cat

from *The Cat's Whiskers*

Words and music by
Peter Thorne
(b. 1955)

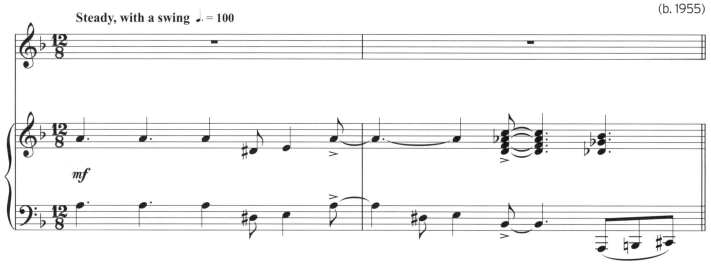

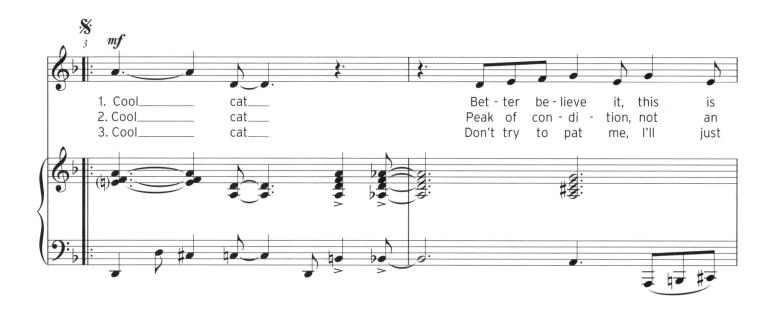

1. Cool_____ cat_____ Bet - ter be - lieve it, this is
2. Cool_____ cat_____ Peak of con - di - tion, not an
3. Cool_____ cat_____ Don't try to pat me, I'll just

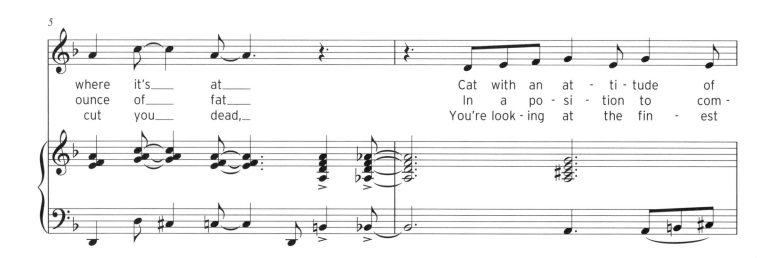

where it's___ at___ Cat with an at - ti - tude of
ounce of___ fat___ In a po - si - tion to com -
cut you___ dead,___ You're look - ing at the fin - est

cold dis - dain,___ a - gain and a - gain___ I
-mand re - spect,___ su - preme - ly se - lect,___ the
quad - ru - ped___ who e - ver was fed___ on

1.
(1.) leave you flat on the mat!___

2.
(2.) per - fect a - ris - to - crat!___ I re -
(3.) fine smoked sal - mon and ham___ You may

-frain from giv - ing af - fec - tion,___ It simp - ly is - n't my style,
say that I'm just an e - go,___ A fly fe - line wan-na - be___

Lyrics visible in the score:

14
But drop a mor - sel in my di - rec - tion,___ And I
But I am here to tell you, A - mi - go;___ If

17a
(2.) just might purr for a while.___

D.S. senza rep.

17b
(3.) Gat - sby was a cat He'd have no - thing on me.___

19
Cool___ cat___ Me - ow___ Cool___ cat___

Prr prr I know that you try___ to be help - ful and kind___ to me,

But you won't find___ me scratch - ing with my___ paw___

on your front door.___ Cool_____ cat,___

don't e - ver doubt it, I'm a Cool_____ cat,___

Teaching notes

Trad. *arr.* Wright   The Gartán Mother's Lullaby   page 2

This traditional song is a lullaby sung by a mother from the Parish of Gartan in County Donegal, Ireland with words set down by Seosamh MacCathmhaoil (Joseph Campbell). There are two references to characters from Irish mythology: 'Sheevra' is a type of Irish fairy and 'Eeval' is the name of the Queen of the Northern Fairies. 'Lianbhan' is an old Irish word for 'little child' and the Green Man is commonly seen as being a symbol of the coming of spring.

A highly atmospheric song, this needs to be sung with a gentle tone and a good sense of the rocking, two-in-a-bar pulse, which will keep the music going without dragging. Although there is little in the way of dynamic contrast marked, think how you can shape the phrases to keep the music alive and interesting. Try to breathe in silently so as not to disturb the mood and ensure that you have plenty of air to sustain each line for its full length as there are some longer notes at the ends of phrases.

A lullaby is a very common theme for songs from all around the world. Can you find other examples to listen to? You could compare them to this one from Ireland and see how other countries have their own interpretations.

Trad. *arr.* Wright   El Vito   page 5

This song is a version of a traditional folk song and dance that comes from the Andalusia region of Spain and it can trace its origins back to the 16th century. Among its characteristics are the $\frac{3}{8}$ metre, the lively and vivacious mood, and the use of the Phrygian mode. The Spanish words, 'real' and 'cuartos' refer to old currency though clearly the character in the song does not have enough of either to consider marriage!

In performance, this song needs to be sung with a confident swagger for despite a lack of funds and clothes that are 'all in tatters', the singer does not lack self-respect. The octave leaps at the beginnings of verses need to be clean and well pitched. Although they are all rising intervals you could try making up your own exercise, incorporating both ascending and descending octaves. Keep a good bounce through the short/long rhythms, maybe adding a slight stress to the first beat of the bar, to suggest the stamping feet of the dancers. Don't worry too much about the Spanish in verse 3 as it is pronounced as it looks on the page and really enjoy the last shout of 'Olé' to finish the song with a flourish.

The Phrygian mode is only one of many different modes. See what you can find out about the use of modes in music and how the Phrygian mode is constructed. You might also like to listen to other versions of 'El Vito'. There are, for example, a number of recordings of solo guitarists playing this music.

Armstrong Gibbs   When I Was One-and-Twenty   page 8

Armstrong Gibbs was a prolific and versatile composer best known for his song writing. Although he lived and worked through a time of great change in western classical music, he remained quite traditional, being influenced by popular and folk song styles. He was very keen to ensure that the words of his songs were given high priority in the song so that their full meaning could be conveyed and one of the characteristics of his word setting is that very often each syllable or word is given a separate note.

This is true in this song, which uses the words of the famous poet, A E Housman. It is a text in which a young person of 21 does not listen to the advice of an older, wiser one about falling in love or 'giving his heart away'. The wiser person explains that it is better to give away money and jewels than to risk getting your heart broken but the younger one does not listen and realises, on reaching the age of 22, that falling in love can be a painful experience.

The music here is relatively simple but you need to make sure that the words are very clear and that all the emotions come across. The changing metre should not impede the flow of the song so feel a strong connection to an underlying pulse. The pauses at the end of verse one and especially at the end of the song should be used to full effect to allow your listeners time to appreciate what has happened. Armstrong Gibbs uses the minor key momentarily at the close to help portray a sense of sadness so be aware of this change as you finish the song.

Do you agree with Armstrong Gibbs that words are very important in a song? Or do you think that the music is more important? See if you can think of different reasons for why one might be more or less important than the other.

Plumstead   Close Thine Eyes   page 11

Mary Plumstead was a 20th-century composer but in this song she chose to set words from the 17th century supposedly by King Charles I. In fact, it is thought that the words were really written by Francis Quares, who was a contemporary of the king.

Perhaps due to their age, the words do seem slightly strange. A 'quiet conscience' is given a personality, as the poem implies that unless 'she' sings, even the music of kings will seem out of tune. The use of 'thy', 'thee' and 'thine' adds to the old-fashioned feel. It is, though, a beautiful song of reassurance, with the singer letting the loved one know that they can sleep safe and sound in the knowledge that they are being guarded by one who never sleeps.

This song should be sung quite slowly though it definitely needs a feeling of two-in-a-bar given the time signature of $\frac{2}{2}$. Try practising it with a slight stress on the second beat in the bar so that you do not fall into the trap of moving the music towards a $\frac{4}{4}$ metre. Don't let the longer held notes in the middle of phrases sag on such words as 'eyes', 'safe' or 'peace' but keep them energised so that they flow into the next half of the phrase each time. There has to be a lovely air of calm and peace in this song but don't be frightened of opening out the voice for the f on the 'mirth of kings'.

This song is not just a solo song but there are also versions for choirs. See if you can find a recording of one to listen to and compare it with your interpretation.

Glanville-Hicks   Come Sleep   page 13

Peggy Glanville-Hicks was a 20th-century Australian composer. She studied composition at the Royal College of Music with Ralph Vaughan Williams and throughout her life she championed contemporary music. She lived in America working as a critic for the *New Herald Tribune* before moving to Greece and finally back to Australia.

The words to 'Come Sleep' are by the playwright and poet John Fletcher who was a contemporary of Shakespeare. They are about someone who is unhappy and so longs to fall asleep and experience the distractions of 'some pleasing dreams' for, although sleep is only a temporary state, at least it provides a means of experiencing some contentment. The final plea that the joy might last is particularly keenly felt.

Counting carefully is the key to this song as the metre keeps changing even, at one point, moving into the unusual time signature of $\frac{1}{4}$. Keep a feeling of the overall flow of the phrases and make sure that you plan where to breathe very carefully as some of the phrases are long. Remember that you always need to shorten the end of a phrase slightly in order to breathe rather than risk being late for the start of the next phrase. Aim for a lovely smooth *legato* throughout this song, letting the natural rise and fall of the musical lines emerge.

There are two other well-known settings of these words by John Fletcher, those of Ivor Gurney and Peter Warlock. See if you can find recordings of these to listen to, to see how other composers have interpreted the words.

| Hyde | The Apple Tree | page 16 |

Miriam Hyde was an Australian composer who was also a concert pianist and a poet. She wrote over 50 songs and always said how important words were to her work.

This very gentle song has three sections that are almost identical before the final last section brings a change. This is to emphasise the poet's feeling that, while the apple tree, the olive tree and the orange tree all listen to her, there is someone who is perhaps not listening so carefully. Between the first and second sections and then again between the second and third there are short piano interludes. Even though you are not singing you must remain 'in the song' to ensure that the atmosphere is not broken. Think about how you might do this with your face and eyes, as this is not the sort of song where big gestures would be appropriate. After the very lyrical lines of the first sections, the rhythm differs in the final part so make sure that you keep this very accurate. Try experimenting too with how long you want to hold the pause in the penultimate phrase. Above all there should be a feeling of poise.

This song was originally written for a harp to accompany the voice. Find a recording of some harp music and, when you have heard the type of sounds it makes, see if you can imagine what this song would sound like with a harp rather than the piano.

| Exley | Peacocks | page 18 |

Judith Exley is from New Zealand and she has always been fascinated by music from Japan and Indonesia, with an especial fondness for the Gamelan and its repertoire.

'Peacocks' is a song in two very different sections, each reflecting the 'voice' of the two different characters, the peacock and the peahen. Both sections make use of a repeated octave motif but in the first part the accompaniment is continuous whereas in the second, the singer is often left alone.

The peacock is a rather pompous bird and his section needs to be sung boldly, in a 'strutting style' as he describes all his beautiful colours. You need to pitch all the octaves very carefully, always thinking over the upper note so that it stays bright and true. There are some moments of dissonance where notes 'clash' but don't be put off by these as they all add to the brash feeling of the boastful bird. Really enjoy the *glissandi*, which allow you to swoop between the notes of the octaves, but do make sure that, after the sliding, you arrive on the correct note. Don't forget to use a seductive tone in the final bar of the peacock's section.

The peahen though is not interested in the peacock's showing off, so when you come to her section, keep the running notes very neat and in tune as you sing almost unaccompanied and aim to convey her interest not in the peacock but in the possibility of dinner.

Can you work out what sort of descending scale is being used in the Peahen's section?

| Cowles | Lurking in the Pond | page 21 |

Colin Cowles is an English musician; perhaps best known for his writings for saxophone although he has over 400 varied compositions to his name. He studied at Trinity College of Music and between 1985 and 2000 was an examiner for the college, travelling to countries as far afield as Australia and Iran.

His compositions are influenced by his love of the countryside and this song, with words by his wife Kathleen, is a fine example of that as it takes a light-hearted look at the goings on of the Pond's inhabitants. As it is based on a 'fast swing', there is a jazzy feel to the whole so quavers need to be swung rather than straight and there are opportunities to 'bend' notes as a jazz singer might.

The words are very important, as you need to convey the different antics of the pond dwellers and the other creatures that fly 'so high in the air'. You could try practising by speaking the words out loud in the rhythms of the song to help you get them neat and projected. Think about ways you could vary your singing too, to suggest the different physical attributes of those that 'stomp' and those that 'fly'. The final 'boo, boo, bi, doo' needs to be very cheeky even though it is sung quietly.

As this song has some elements of jazz style you may like to have a listen to some other recordings of jazz singers in a fast swing style.

| Chilcott | Irish Blessing | page 25 |

As a boy and then again as a student, Bob Chilcott sang in the choir of King's College, Cambridge. He now combines a busy career as a well-known composer and conductor working with many choirs including the BBC Singers.

The words of the 'Irish Blessing' are part of an ancient Irish prayer. In Celtic literature, images of nature and everyday life are often used to express a feeling of spirituality and here the wind, sun and rain all form part of the blessing being invoked. There are two verses that seem to be virtually the same but look at the performance directions to help achieve contrasts of expression. Listen to the piano part to see how it changes between the verses as this too adds a different colour to the whole. You need to sing the quicker notes on the word 'fields' with great care and clarity and make sure that you have planned how much air you will need to sustain the longer notes, especially those at the ends of phrases. Notice how, as the song finishes, it gets gradually slower and quieter so think how you can really use the composer's markings to establish a lovely peaceful and reflective mood at the close.

Singing quietly is often more of a challenge than singing loudly. Why do you think that this is and can you think of some exercises that you could practise that will help you with this work?

| Harris | Villanelle | page 28 |

Paul Harris is a world-renowned music educator with numerous publications to his name. He studied clarinet, composition and conducting at the Royal Academy of Music in London.

The title of this song, 'Villanelle', refers to a particular style of poem, which seems to have developed in France as early as the 16th century. It has a strict form, based around three-line sections and uses just two rhyming sounds at the ends of lines. In this song the sounds are 'yawl' from the first line and 'sea' from the second.

A 'yawl' is a sailing ship with two masts and here its cargo is liquorice, which comes from the root of a plant and has a distinctive, sweet flavour. Liquorice was widely traded by sea in the 18th and 19th centuries and the main character in this song is an old sailor from those times, looking back at his sea voyages, when he sailed through sudden storms or 'squalls' and remembering his friends who are gone.

In the first section of the song the phrases rise and fall like the waves of the sea and you need to think how you can shape your singing to convey this, taking care to pitch the sometimes awkward intervals very carefully. Be aware too of how the arpeggio figures in the piano are also suggesting the sea's movement. Think of how you can communicate the sounds of the 'thundering' sea and the 'mermaid's call'. The second half of the song has some big climatic moments so make sure that the voice is not pushed but remains open and free as you sing more loudly. Think too about whether the emotions of the old sailor change as the song comes to a quieter ending.

Liquorice has a very distinctive taste which some people like and some people hate. If you have never tried it then perhaps see if you can find a liquorice sweet and give it a go!

The words for this song are from a collection of poems called *A Child's Garden of Verse* by the famous 19th-century Scottish author, Robert Louis Stephenson. Perhaps best known for his novels, *Treasure Island*, *Kidnapped* and *The Strange Case of Dr Jekyll and Mr Hyde*, Stephenson was also interested in music, playing the piano and composing.

The contemporary composer, Ian Higginson is known for the rhythmic vitality of his music and this song certainly calls for a high level of energy and crisp diction in order to portray all the different pictures seen from the speeding train. Practise this song slowly at first, to make sure that every note is sung right through the centre, particularly in the passages where there are semitones. As you get quicker you need to think about your breathing, making sure that you take on air very quickly so that the forward movement of the music is not interrupted. The ending needs to be very clear too even though it is very quiet. You want to leave your listeners with the feeling that all the sights really have 'gone for ever'.

When you are next on a fast journey by train or car see if you can describe all the things you see flashing past your window. Could you make up some rhythms to fit your words and to suggest the speed you are travelling?

Thorne   Cool Cat   page 36

Peter Thorne studied music at Oxford University and he has a life long love of jazz. He likes to combine jazz and classical elements in his compositions, putting in unexpected twists to suggest a mood.

In 'Cool Cat' he has set his own words to music in an upbeat number, which really reflects the character of this 'cat with an attitude'. You need to sing this with great confidence, acting out the personality of this feline who commands respect and doesn't give affection lightly. Facial expression as well as different vocal qualities will be needed to make an effective performance. Before singing read the words out loud seeing how you can use your voice to portray the mood. When you sing think how you can use some of these effects to communicate to your listeners, thinking especially how you will manage the 'me-ow' and the 'prr prr' towards the end. There are also a number of off-beat accents in the song so work on defining these very clearly as they give real impetus to the song.

Practising in front of a mirror is a good idea to make sure that you are acting with the face and eyes as you sing. This will help you 'inhabit' the character. You may have a cat as a pet or know someone who does so try and watch how cats move and behave. Or find a video of a cat behaving in an aloof manner and see if there are any of its actions or expressions that you could use to enhance your performance when you are singing.